Profiles in American History

The Life and Times of

JAMES MADISON

Mitchell Lane
PUBLISHERS

P.O. Box 196 · Hockessin, Delaware 19707

Titles in the Series

The Life and Times of

Abigail Adams
Alexander Hamilton
Benjamin Franklin
Betsy Ross
The Brothers Custer: Galloping to Glory
Clara Barton
Eli Whitney
Father Jacques Marquette
George Rogers Clark
Hernando Cortés
James Madison
John Adams
John Cabot
John Hancock
John Paul Jones
John Peter Zenger
Nathan Hale
Patrick Henry
Paul Revere
Peter Stuyvesant
Rosa Parks
Samuel Adams
Sir Walter Raleigh
Stephen F. Austin
Susan B. Anthony
Thomas Jefferson
William Penn

The Life and Times of

JAMES MADISON

Barbara Somervill

Printing   1   2   3   4   5   6   7   8   9

Library of Congress Cataloging-in-Publication Data

Somervill, Barbara A.
  The life and times of James Madison / by Barbara Somervill.
      p. cm. — (Profiles in American history)
  Includes bibliographical references and index.
  Audience: Grades 7-8.
  ISBN 978-1-58415-530-0 (library bound)
 1. Madison, James, 1751–1836—Juvenile literature.
2. Presidents—United States—Biography—Juvenile literature. 3. United States—History—Revolution, 1775–1783—Juvenile literature. 4. United States—Politics and government—1775–1783—Juvenile literature. 5. United States—Politics and government—1783–1809—Juvenile literature. I. Title.
E342.S66 2008
973.5'1092—dc22
[B]
                                                                                                2007000790

ABOUT THE AUTHOR: Barbara Somervill is a working writer and a lifelong learner. Her writing has taken her through several careers: journalism, teaching, drama, corporate communications, educational textbook writing, and nonfiction children's writing. Ms. Somervill has had more than 75 books published. This is her second book for Mitchell Lane Publishers. Ms. Somervill is an avid bridge player and loves theater reading. She lives in South Carolina with her husband and is a mother and grandmother.

PHOTO CREDITS: Cover, pp. 1, 8, 14, 28, 36—Getty Images; pp. 3, 6, 22, 23, 24, 38, 41—Library of Congress; p. 31—Sharon Beck.

PUBLISHER'S NOTE: This story is based on the author's extensive research, which she believes to be accurate. Documentation of such research is contained on page 45.

    The internet sites referenced herein were active as of the publication date. Due to the fleeting nature of some web sites, we cannot guarantee they will all be active when you are reading this book.

                                                                                                PLB

Profiles in American History

Contents

*For Your Information

James Madison (1751–1836) was the fourth president of the United States. He spent decades helping to write and then champion the U.S. Constitution and its first ten amendments, the Bill of Rights.

CHAPTER 1

A Wartime President

President James Madison sank lower into the carriage seat and rubbed a hand through his thinning hair. His bones ached from fatigue and he felt sick at heart. Madison had spent the day on a bloody battlefield just a few miles northeast of Washington, D.C., watching his ragtag American troops get routed by the invading British. The booming of cannons and the screams of wounded and dying soldiers had been sickening.

The president was not a young man at sixty-three, but he had been on horseback for most of the day. At one point during the battle in Bladensburg, Maryland, he had taken command of one of the few remaining American batteries. He was the first and only president to exercise his authority as commander in chief during a battle.

Now his carriage bounced over a rough dirt road, deeper into Virginia. He knew that behind him, British troops were pouring into the undefended capital. His home, the President's House, had been left empty. Thank goodness his beautiful wife Dolley had fled to safety earlier that day. During the battle, he'd scribbled a note and had it delivered to her by horseback. It told Dolley that things weren't looking good for the Americans. She should collect his important cabinet papers and run. He would meet her in Virginia the next day.

Dolley Madison fled the White House mere hours before British troops invaded in August 1814. She ordered servants to load a cart with a portrait of George Washington, her husband's cabinet papers, and important pieces of silver.

Other people fleeing Washington peered at Madison as he passed them in his carriage. Some recognized the president and muttered angrily. Others cursed him openly. It was his fault that the United States was in this blasted war with the British in the first place. It had even been called "Mr. Madison's War" by some of his enemies.

Madison kept his chin up. At only five-foot-four and a hundred pounds, he was small, but he knew his courage had to be huge for what lay ahead. The Americans had been defeated badly that day, but the War of 1812 wasn't over yet.

When the American Revolution ended in 1783, the problems between the infant United States and Great Britain did not end. Great Britain refused to retreat from American land on the Great Lakes. The United States simply could not force the British from their land without starting another war. The American Revolution had been expensive; the new nation had heavy debts to pay.

In addition, setting up a new nation required tremendous planning and energy. The country needed its own currency, postal system, army, navy, roads, and laws. The nation needed a form of government, which first appeared under the Articles of Confederation. Later, the government would be set down in the United States Constitution. Developing, writing, changing, and passing that document took not days or months, but years.

In the early 1800s, Great Britain dominated the oceans. Britain, in an on-and-off war with France, tried to blockade Europe, America's marketplace. If America were to prosper, merchants had to be able to sell their goods there. The British had a different idea. British ships stopped American merchant vessels and either seized cargoes or turned the ships away. The British looked through the American crews and took any sailors considered to be British. Following a practice called impressment, the British navy forced these sailors to work on their vessels. They claimed that if a sailor was born in England, it meant he was British. They didn't care if the sailors had become American citizens.

Americans were outraged. Why were they still having problems with the British? Many remembered the hardships of the American Revolution. Some had lost fathers, husbands, friends, or other relatives in the war. There were those who accused the British of being little more than pirates. For the most part, New Englanders

wanted to avoid war at all costs—but at the same time, merchants could not afford to lose ships, cargoes, and men.

In 1807, the British frigate *Leopard* fired on the USS *Chesapeake* off the coast of Virginia. Three men died in the scuffle, and the British impressed four seamen. America reacted by passing a law that banned trade with England and France in 1809. That law was short-lived, and trade with Britain reopened in 1810. Again, the British seized American trade ships, citizens, and cargoes.

Americans turned to their leader for a solution. President Madison had to weigh several factors. Should the nation risk going to war again? Could the United States win another war against Great Britain? How could the country pay for an expensive war? Would the states support the federal government in this action? Madison asked the Congress to support a build up of the army and navy in 1811. Congress agreed to give money to the army, but the navy got nothing.

Madison still hoped to find a peaceful solution that would keep the United States from going to war. Great Britain wasn't cooperating. He wrote to Thomas Jefferson in February 1812: "[A]ll that we see from G. B. [Great Britain] indicates an adherence to her mad policy towards the U.S."[1]

On June 18, 1812, Madison asked Congress to pass a declaration of war against the British. In a letter to the Senate and House of Representatives, Madison wrote, "British cruisers have been in the continued practice of violating the American flag on the great highway of nations, and of seizing and carrying off persons sailing under it. . . . [Because of this practice] thousands of American citizens, under the safeguard of public law and of their national flag, have been torn from their country and from everything dear to them."[2]

Congress agreed. The United States was at war with Great Britain.

The American battle plan focused on taking Canada from Great Britain in three sections: Lake Champlain to Montreal, across the Niagara region, and Canadian territory across from Detroit. For the war to be a success, the United States needed to stop attacks by Native Americans along the Great Lakes. It also had to safeguard markets for American products.

The war effort struggled from the beginning. Connecticut and Massachusetts refused to send men to fight. In July the U.S. port of Michilimackinac surrendered to the British without firing a shot. America's General William Hull, having advanced into Canada, retreated with 2,200 troops to Detroit. America's Fort Dearborn in Michigan was attacked and burned. One highlight in the otherwise bleak war news was the USS *Constitution*'s victory over the British ship *Guerriere.*

The British counterattacked along Lake Champlain and the Hudson River in an effort to cut New England off from the other states. Other attacks took place in New Orleans and along the Mississippi. The British established a blockade of the Chesapeake Bay, barring commercial travel into Baltimore and Washington. Over the next two years, battles raged on land and sea. The United States chalked up wins and losses.

In August 1814, the British ranks swelled as troops no longer needed for the war against France joined the Canadian forces. While the Americans fended off a frenzied attack in New York's Lake Champlain area, the British navy sailed into the Chesapeake Bay. In Washington, D.C., Madison worked furiously to organize a defense of the capital. When it became obvious that the British would invade and the battle of Bladensburg was lost, Madison fled.

Over 4,000 British troops swarmed into America's capital city. They burned the President's House—which would be named the White House after it was repaired and given a fresh coat of paint. They also burned the Capitol and several other government buildings before retreating to their ships and attacking Baltimore. It was during the bombing of Baltimore that Francis Scott Key wrote a poem that would later be known as the lyrics to the national anthem, "The Star-Spangled Banner."

Madison returned to Washington two days after the initial attack. The Madisons lived in temporary housing while the White House was under repair. Madison immediately ordered that the Post Office and the Patent Office buildings be converted for the Congress to use. The president also fired John Armstrong Jr., the secretary of war, for not defending Washington, D.C., from the British. Armstrong was replaced by James Monroe.

In the battle of New Orleans, General Andrew Jackson led his outnumbered U.S. forces of soldiers, local militiamen, free African Americans, Choctaw Indians, and French pirates to victory against the British. Herbert Morton Stoops's painting shows how U.S. troops took cover behind earthworks and picked off oncoming British troops.

By late 1814, Madison was eager for the war to end. He sent diplomats to discuss a ceasefire and end to the war. The Treaty of Ghent was signed in December. The most demanding crisis of Madison's presidency had come to an end.

News of the war's end did not travel quickly. In 1815 the British attacked New Orleans, and Andrew Jackson's troops fought valiantly. One of the greatest American victories of the War of 1812, the battle of New Orleans, came after the war had been declared over.

The USS *Constitution*

The USS Constitution *in 1997*

The timbers creaked as the USS *Constitution* cut through the rough Atlantic waters southeast of Halifax, Nova Scotia. From the topmast came the call, "Sail ho! Sou' by sou'east!" The sailor had spotted the HMS *Guerriere,* a frigate in the service of the British navy.

Isaac Hull was the commander of the *Constitution,* a 44-gun frigate and one of the original six ships of the United States Navy. A crew of 450 manned the sails and guns of the ship known as "Old Ironsides." The ship had earned its nickname because cannonballs bounced off its thick oak sides.

The *Guerriere* faced overwhelming odds. It was outmanned and outgunned, but its commander, Captain James R. Dacres, was itching for a fight. He had faith in the training and reputation of the British navy.

The two ships met in battle on August 19, 1812. *Guerriere* fired one broadside, then another. The cannonballs missed their targets. *Constitution* responded, firing from its forward guns. It raked the enemy's hull and masts as the two ships closed on each other. *Guerriere*'s mizzenmast fell. Then its bowsprit—the pole extending from the prow—became entangled in *Constitution*'s rigging. The crews entered into hand-to-hand combat; the *Constitution* emerged victorious. The *Guerriere* suffered severe damage during the battle and was set on fire and blown up; *Constitution* captured the survivors.

This was one of America's major sea victories in the War of 1812. By 1830, the *Constitution* had passed its prime, and the United States Navy wanted to get rid of it. Popular opinion saved the *Constitution.* The ship has been rebuilt several times, including in 1997 in honor of her 200th birthday. The modern "Old Ironsides" is the oldest commissioned ship in the navy, with a crew of fifty-five sailors and a commissioned naval officer as her captain.

James Madison was born into a family that could afford to give him a private tutor and then an education at the College of New Jersey at Princeton. The young Madison loved college, but he worked so hard at his studies that he feared he was becoming ill. This fear of illness plagued him throughout his very long life.

CHAPTER 2

A Childhood of Privilege

James Madison's ancestor, John Madison, immigrated to the Virginia Colony from Europe in 1653. Like most colonists, John Madison lived in an area plagued by mosquitoes, yellow fever, and malaria in the summer months.

Three generations of the Madison family followed John's. In 1723, Ambrose Madison (James Madison's grandfather) and Thomas Chew were given a 4,675-acre parcel of land in the nearby Piedmont region by James Taylor, father of the women Ambrose and Thomas had married. Ambrose was socially well connected and a member of Virginia's upper class. To get permanent title to the property, he had three years to clear the land, build a house, and establish a plantation of some type.

Although the house was built, Ambrose and his wife, Frances Taylor Madison, did not move to Mount Pleasant, their half of the land, until 1732. The land was made up of rolling hills thick with hickory, pine, poplar, red and white oak, dogwood, and chestnut trees. Local farms produced corn, barley, wheat, and hay. The Orange County neighborhood had a number of wealthy families, including the Taylors and the Chews.

Within six months of moving, Ambrose died from poisoning. The poison was slow acting, and Ambrose suffered a prolonged death. Three slaves were accused and convicted of poisoning their master.

One was executed and the other two were whipped and returned to Madison's estate. Frances was left to run the plantation on her own, which she managed with remarkable success.

Once Frances's oldest son James became an adult, he helped her run the property. By this time, the Madisons had built a prosperous farm. They kept pigs, chickens, and cattle. They grew much of their own food. James was a respected member of the vestry of the local Anglican Church. This was an important position in the community because vestrymen were expected to enforce strict codes of morality. Drunkenness or use of foul language was severely punished. Madison's position in the community was similar to that of a local judge.

In 1749, James married Nelly Conway, and two years later, on March 16, 1751, the Madisons had their first of twelve children, James Junior. Over the next ten years, the family built a huge house. The plantation was still called Mount Pleasant; the name Montpelier would not be used until 1780. After James was born, other Madison babies followed at roughly two-year intervals: Francis in 1753; Ambrose in 1755; Catlett, who died as an infant, in 1758; and Nelly in 1760. William, Sarah, and Elizabeth followed. Brother Reuben arrived after James Junior had left for college.

Life on the plantation followed the seasons. Spring was for plowing and planting; summer for raising vegetables and cash crops. The fall brought harvest time; the winter was a fallow season. The Madisons used slave labor to work their farm. This was a common practice on southern plantations and acceptable among the wealthy. The Virginia Piedmont remained rugged, wild, and somewhat dangerous. The area still suffered from Native American attacks.

Families were caught between two difficult decisions. If they kept their children with them in the Piedmont, they risked death from Indian attacks. If they sent their children to the coast, they risked death from disease. The Madisons decided to keep their children with them, but even there disease threatened. From 1755 to 1757, smallpox swept through the Ohio Valley and down into Virginia. People knew enough about smallpox to keep healthy people away from the sick, but many people died of the dreaded disease.

Little is known of James Madison's young childhood other than that he was small and sickly. He began his education at home with

a tutor, which was typical for the children of a wealthy Virginia plantation family. In 1754, Madison's father hired John Bricky as schoolmaster. Six years later, the neighborhood pooled their money to hire Kelly Jennings to educate the local children. Students learned reading, writing, and arithmetic. They copied poetry and learned how to dance.

At eleven years old, James went away to boarding school. This was no hardship for the eager, gifted student. His teacher was Donald Robertson, a young man educated in Scotland. Over the next five years, James learned English, Latin, algebra, geometry, geography, French, Italian, and Greek and Roman history. In 1767, James left Robertson's school for two years of home tutoring and lessons with brothers Francis, Ambrose, and William, and sister Nelly.

By the age of eighteen, most wealthy young men in the colonies were well into their first year of college. James Madison was not. Most young men in Virginia attended the College of William and Mary. James Madison did not. By the time he was ready for college, William and Mary had developed a poor reputation. At any rate, the school was in the Tidewater, and James's sickly nature could not endure summer months in that region. Instead James went to the relatively new College of New Jersey at Princeton. Serious and bookish, Madison packed his bags, along with his tutor Thomas Martin, Martin's brother Alexander, and a servant named Sawney. The trip from the Madisons' plantation to Princeton took about ten days of hard travel.

James immediately "tested out" of his freshman year. In 1769 a student could take a series of exams and skip a year if he passed. James began his college education as a sophomore, living in Princeton's Nassau Hall. Always studious and fascinated by books, James looked forward to his next three years of study as a true opportunity. He wrote to a friend: "I am perfectly pleased with my present situation; and the prospect before me of three years confinement, however terrible it may sound, has nothing in it, but what will be greatly [eased] by the advantages I hope to derive from it."[1]

Nassau Hall served as a housing facility, lecture hall, dining hall, and library. Built in 1756, Nassau Hall's third floor housed 147 students in rather crowded conditions. The second floor had a dining room on one side and a library on the other. Classes were held

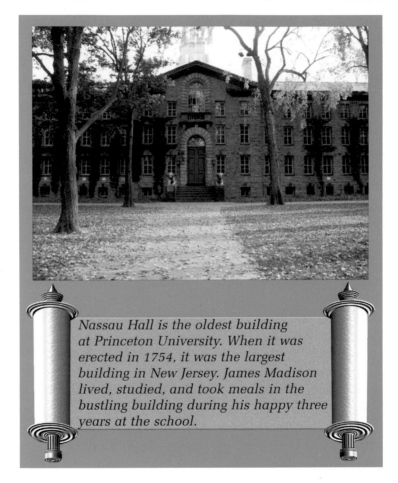

Nassau Hall is the oldest building at Princeton University. When it was erected in 1754, it was the largest building in New Jersey. James Madison lived, studied, and took meals in the bustling building during his happy three years at the school.

in the lecture hall on the first floor. Madison started college in 1769 and graduated in 1771, a fully educated young man of twenty. He returned home without a clue as to what he'd do with himself.

James was physically exhausted. He'd worked so hard at Princeton that he risked his health. Back home, he rested, taught his younger siblings, and read a great deal. Times were changing, and the colonies were on the brink of revolution. The very idea of revolution thrilled Madison, who had decided to dedicate his life to public service. He could not have chosen a better time. Madison was only twenty-five in 1776 when the colonies signed the Declaration of Independence. The budding nation needed someone with the young Madison's learning and intelligence.

Slavery in the South

Slavery was not a new idea when traders brought Africans to the colonies and sold them into bondage. Many ancient cultures—Rome, Greece, Egypt, and China, for example—built their greatness on the backs of slave labor. Long before a Dutch trader sold twenty Africans to Virginians at Jamestown in 1619, Europeans sold captured Africans at slave markets in the Caribbean and South America. During the years when the slave trade flourished, roughly a half million Africans were sold in North American slave markets. This was a small fraction of the nearly 13 million Africans sold to work South American gold and silver mines and Caribbean sugarcane fields.

Slavery in the colonies did not become popular until the 1700s. At that time, major slave markets existed in every colony, but the largest were in New York, Boston, and Charleston. Slaves in the earlier colonies were considered more like regular workers and less like property.

In the northern colonies, from Pennsylvania to Massachusetts, the business of selling humans into slavery met with open resistance. Quakers and Puritans would not accept the idea of slavery; it went against their religious beliefs. In the South, African slave labor became the economic base for large southern plantations. Slaves married and produced children, who belonged to the slave owner, according to the law of the day. Active birth rates guaranteed a fresh supply of free labor. Since prices paid for raw cotton, tobacco, rice, and indigo varied greatly, a grower needed to make as much profit as possible.

The slave trade slowed down after the 1770s. Rhode Island became the first colony to ban the importation of slaves in 1774. Other states, such as Massachusetts, New Jersey, and Pennsylvania, followed. While the ban ended the practice of bringing new slaves into the colony, it did not free those slaves already there.

Slaves on a Virginia Plantation

In 1776, when the Declaration of Independence was signed, many of the nation's Founding Fathers owned slaves. This included James Madison, Thomas Jefferson, and George Washington.

For Your Information

Colonists rebelled against a tax-happy British government that tried to take advantage of their love of tea. Dressed as Native Americans, about 200 men dumped the cargo of three ships into the Boston Harbor. This rebellion sparked the fire of activism in a young James Madison.

CHAPTER
3

From Revolution to the Bill of Rights

From the time he left college, James Madison made government and politics his primary interests. At home, he scoured volumes on the great governments in history. In 1773, a group of rebels heaved a shipload of tea into Boston Harbor. Madison, normally quiet and shy, instantly became a political activist. He joined protests against the domineering rule of the British. Out of the family library rose an avid rebel.

As the colonies built an army under General George Washington, Madison trained the local militia in Orange County. In the American Revolution, colonial militia faced a more powerful, better-armed British army. Many officers on the American side had limited experience in combat situations. It was not unusual that someone like Madison, with no actual military training, would be responsible for training militia.

In 1776, the same year that the Declaration of Independence was signed, Orange County elected Madison to represent this area at the Virginia convention. At a meeting in Williamsburg, Madison agreed to serve on a committee to draft a declaration of rights for the Virginia constitution. It was in Williamsburg that Madison first met Thomas Jefferson. The two would not become close until 1779 when Jefferson was governor of the state, but the basis for their friendship was laid. Both men were well-educated, avid readers,

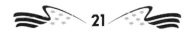

Five men were on the committee assigned to write a Declaration of Independence for America: (left to right) Thomas Jefferson, John Adams, Benjamin Franklin, Robert Livingston, and Roger Sherman.

and intelligent. They were landowners who became respected political powers. Throughout the American Revolution, Jefferson and Madison worked to ensure that military supplies reached the southern colonial troops.

Madison made quite an impression on the General Assembly and on Thomas Jefferson. Jefferson admired Madison for "the powers and polish of his pen."[1] There was no question of Madison's knowledge of politics. His entire education had led to his expertise. Madison was a politician who did his homework.

In 1777 James Madison lost the election for a seat in the Virginia legislature. However, the House of Delegates chose him to become a member of the eight-man Council of State. That body advised the governor and was considered part of Virginia's executive body.

The meeting of the General Assembly of the Continental Congress in 1779 brought both Jefferson and Madison to Philadelphia. The two roomed at the same boardinghouse, ate meals together, and debated the future of the new nation. They formed a solid friendship and a partnership during that month at Congress.

One of the tasks they took on jointly was founding a national library. Madison, as chairman of the committee, recommended that the new Library of Congress should have more than 1,300 volumes. The books on the list would cover political history, law, treaties, and information on diplomacy. Unfortunately Congress soundly defeated Madison's recommendations for the new library. The library was too expensive.

The bachelor Madison took time off from his political work to court a young lady, the daughter of his colleague William Floyd. Catherine "Kitty" Floyd was sixteen years old when thirty-one-year-old Madison took an interest in her. Madison proposed marriage and Catherine accepted. The engagement lasted only a few months before Catherine called it off. Little wonder, since Madison was remarkably short, shy, and withdrawn. He was also either sickly or a hypochondriac. Government and his personal health occupied most of his time.

Madison was in Philadelphia when the new states devised a loosely framed document that set out their government. Drafted in 1777 but not passed until 1781, the Articles of Confederation set up a

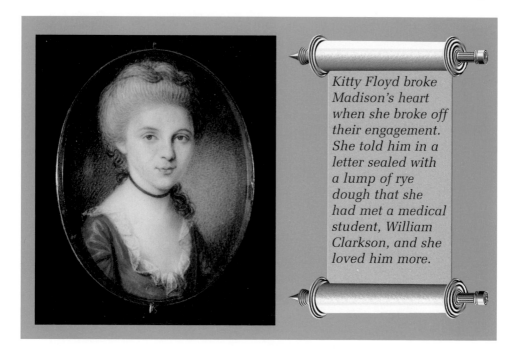

Kitty Floyd broke Madison's heart when she broke off their engagement. She told him in a letter sealed with a lump of rye dough that she had met a medical student, William Clarkson, and she loved him more.

strong cooperation between states. The document originally planned for a powerful federal government. However, individual states complained about giving too much power to a federal government. The problem was that larger states wanted more power, and smaller states felt they would have no voice. Northern states had one outlook on trade; southern states looked at trade differently. The plan for a powerful central government became so watered down that the Articles of Confederation were nearly useless.

Patrick Henry, best known for his "Give me liberty or give me death" speech, didn't like Madison's politics. He did everything he could to keep Madison from getting elected to the Senate.

Madison listened to all arguments. He heard the merchants rant about their need for a federal government that could develop trade agreements with other nations. He understood that the advantages merchants had enjoyed under British rule had disappeared. It was obvious that the loosely arranged government would not be able to function.

The Articles of Confederation were failing, and many political leaders of the United States realized they needed a stronger government. This was the foundation for writing the United States Constitution, a document that set up the government in three clearly defined branches. This was Madison's greatest strength. He had studied every republic, every government, and every political philosophy available in books.

Much of the Constitution came from Madison's ideas of what a democratic government should be. As a result, many people called Madison the "Father of the Constitution," a title he did not like. He wrote in a letter to William Cogswell much later, "You give me a credit to which I have no claim, in calling me 'the writer of the Constitution of the United States.' This was not, like the fabled Goddess of Wisdom, the offspring of a single brain. It ought to be regarded as the work of many heads and many hands."[2]

Madison asked Thomas Jefferson, at the time the American ambassador in Paris, what his views were about the proposed Constitution. For the most part, Jefferson approved of the way the government would be set up, however, he did not like " . . . the omission of a bill of rights providing clearly and without the aid of [explanations] for freedom of religion, freedom of the press, protection against standing armies . . . "[3] Madison agreed and responded, "My own opinion has always been in favor of a bill of rights provided it be so framed as not to imply powers not meant to be included in the [list]."[4]

A great deal of effort went into promoting the proposed Constitution. To be approved, the document would be reviewed, debated, and voted on by each state. Madison argued for a stronger federal government by writing essays, along with Alexander Hamilton and John Jay; the essays were published as *The Federalist*. Madison worked for passage at the Virginia Constitutional Convention, and Virginia became the tenth state to ratify the U.S. Constitution.

In the 1788 election following the passage of the Constitution, Madison ran for a seat in the Senate. Unfortunately for Madison, Patrick Henry held tremendous power in the Virginia legislature. Henry was an Anti-federalist, a person who believed in a weak central government and powerful state governments. Quite simply, Henry did not like Madison's politics. Patrick Henry thwarted Madison's Senate bid, supporting Richard Henry Lee and William Grayson, two other Anti-federalists.

Madison then ran for the new House of Representatives and succeeded. Patrick Henry tried to block Madison's election there, too, by persuading James Monroe to run against Madison. Madison's supporters would not be defeated. They pushed people into voting, even carrying a sick man from his bed to the polls. Unfortunately that man voted for Monroe. However Madison still won, earning 1,308 votes to Monroe's 972. Madison quickly became a respected member of the House of Representatives. Fellow Congressman Fisher Adams of Massachusetts described Madison: "He is possessed of a sound judgment, which perceives truth with great clearness, and can trace it through the mazes of debate, without losing it. . . . "[5]

Part of the agreement that allowed the Constitution to be passed in some states was the development of a Bill of Rights that protected every citizen. These rights would be amendments to the Constitution. Madison wrote, "The people of many states, have thought it necessary to raise barriers against power in all forms and departments of government. . . . "[6] He was a natural choice to write the Bill of Rights.

And so, the first ten amendments to the Constitution were added. These ten amendments guaranteed personal rights of free speech, religion, and press. Citizens' homes could not be searched without a warrant, nor could people be arrested without cause. Citizens who were accused of crimes were entitled to a speedy trial by a jury of their peers.

Today these freedoms cover all citizens; however, it is important to remember that not all people were considered equal in the late 1780s. Women could neither vote nor serve on a jury. A slave counted as only three-fifths of a person. Further, only property-owning men could vote. Over time, more amendments have been added to the Constitution, expanding the freedoms and privileges of American citizens.

The Bill of Rights

"Founding Fathers"

In the summer of 1787, representatives from the thirteen fledgling members of the United States met to write a constitution. That document set out the workings of the new federal government. There would be an executive branch, a representative legislature, and a judicial branch. The document outlined how the government would work, but it left off a major consideration: the rights of individual citizens.

The Founding Fathers immediately began working on a solution, a list of rights. Said Thomas Jefferson, "[A] bill of rights is what the people are entitled to against every government on earth . . . and what no just government should refuse."[7] Jefferson may have inspired the Bill of Rights, but James Madison wrote the rough draft.

Madison's document listed the ten basic freedoms that the Founding Fathers cherished. These laws offered many guarantees that would protect individuals from the government and were based on problems that had occurred when Great Britain ruled the colonies.

These are some of the rights that appear in the Bill of Rights:

- Freedom to follow one's own religion
- Freedom of the press and speech
- Freedom to petition the government to start or stop some action and to meet with others to discuss those ideas
- Privacy and protection from the government seizing people, papers, or belongings without a warrant
- Equal status before the law
- The right to a quick and speedy trial, and a trial by jury
- The right to refuse to house soldiers, to join a militia, and to bear arms
- Freedom from excessive punishment for petty crimes

The Bill of Rights makes up the first ten amendments to the United States Constitution. They were adopted in 1791 and became law at that time.

For Your Information

Dolley Madison was a colorful figure who loved wearing turbans with feathers and throwing warm, welcoming White House parties featuring delicious food and sparkling conversation. She was an attractive, intelligent woman with an excellent knowledge of politics and current events.

CHAPTER
4

The Nation's Fourth President

James Madison represented Virginia at the second session of the First Federal Congress in 1790. Alexander Hamilton proposed that the federal government assume states' debts from the American Revolution. Madison opposed the idea. He knew that some states, like Virginia, had already paid most of their debts, and he didn't think it fair for those that had paid to assume the debts of those that hadn't. Many members of Congress agreed.

Another proposal brought up a possible location for a permanent capital city. Madison favored a site along the Potomac River, which would be roughly in the middle of the original thirteen states. To ensure the Potomac site would be accepted, Madison agreed that Philadelphia could serve as a temporary capital until 1800.

Over the next few years, Madison was reelected to the House of Representatives. He complained actively about the British practice of impressment and Britain's seizure of more than 250 American ships in the French West Indies. The problems with the British control of the high seas eventually led to war.

In 1794 long-term bachelor James Madison met the delightful Dolley Payne Todd. Mrs. Todd, recently widowed, was seventeen years younger than the smitten Madison. He was so taken with the lovely, vivacious Dolley that a friend wrote to her, "To being, he thinks so much of you in the day that he has Lost his Tongue, at night he Dreames of you and Starts in his Sleep a Calling on you

to relieve his Flame for he Burns to such an excess that he will be shortly consumed, and he hopes that your Heart will be calous to every other swain but himself."[1]

The whirlwind courtship lasted only a few months. Madison and Dolley married at Harewood, her sister's home in Jefferson County (in today's West Virginia), on September 15, 1794. Madison added more than just a wife to his household, as Dolley's son Payne Todd and her sister Anna came to live with them.

Shortly after the wedding, the pair returned to Philadelphia, where they rented the house previously occupied by James Monroe and his family. The Madisons needed furniture, and James wrote to the Monroes, now in Paris, asking them to purchase quality secondhand furniture for them. European prices on household goods at that time were far cheaper than American prices, and the Madisons trusted the Monroes to buy nice items: carpets, curtains, china, and small furnishings.

By 1797 Madison was ready to retire. He'd had enough of politics and refused to run for reelection again. The family moved to Montpelier to begin remodeling the house. The new doorway followed a design by Madison's good friend Thomas Jefferson. The Monroes shipped excellent furniture to fill the house. Madison asked Jefferson's help in ordering materials and hardware for building the house. The Madisons purchased more than 100,000 nails from Jefferson's nailworks; Jefferson purchased and shipped 190 glass panes and brass door hinges for his friend. Madison became the gentleman farmer, while Dolley entertained guests.

In 1801 Thomas Jefferson took the oath of office as president of the United States. Madison's comfortable days in retirement came to an end when Jefferson appointed him secretary of state. Times were difficult for Madison: His father had died and he had to resolve issues of the estate. In addition, Madison suffered from rheumatism. Still, Jefferson called, and more than twenty years of friendship could not be ignored.

When the Madisons first arrived in Washington, D.C., they stayed with the Jeffersons in the White House. Within weeks they had rented their own home on F Street NW, about two blocks from the White House. As secretary of state, Madison dealt with foreign nations and became involved in the event that doubled the size of the United States: the Louisiana Purchase.

The Louisiana Purchase was the acquisition by the U.S. of 828,000 square miles of French territory, shown in green, in 1803. The cost was a mere $23 million, which came to less than a penny per acre.

By 1804 the problems between the United States and Great Britain had increased. Madison protested, but the English were not particularly interested. Madison said, "I fear they will put our patience to the proof. [They are] making our ports also stations for cruising from. . . . It seems to me that we shall be obliged to have a battery or two in our principal seaports, and to require [foreign] armed vessels to lie under them."[2]

Madison knew that the British government would ignore protests from the American government. The situation was grim. Hundreds of American ships had been lost, along with millions of dollars in cargo. Sailors had been killed in the act of seizing the ships, and others had been abducted and forced to work on British ships. The attack of the British frigate *Leopard* on the USS *Chesapeake* in 1807 was typical of the British abuses on the high seas. The *Leopard* fired on the American ship, killed three men, and impressed four others.

In 1808 James Madison was elected to the presidency. He received 122 electoral votes to Charles Pinckney's 47 and DeWitt Clinton's 6 votes. The inauguration was set for March 4, 1809. In his inaugural address, Madison pointed out, "The present situation of the world is indeed without a parallel, and that of our own country full of difficulties."[3] He said his main goal was to "cherish peace and friendly intercourse with all nations"[4] having similar desires.

Immediately after Madison took the oath of office, Dolley held a party at their home. She wore a simple dress with a long train and a plain neckline, and a purple velvet bonnet. She was, said Margaret Bayard Smith, "all dignity, grace, and affability."[5] The couple danced at the inaugural ball that night, and all eyes were on Dolley. They made an odd couple. Madison was short, thin, and much older; Dolley was charming, pretty, and significantly younger.

Louisa Adams, the wife of John Quincy Adams, described the two:

> Mr. Madison was a very small man in this person, with a very large head—his manners were peculiarly unassuming; and his conversation lively, often playful . . .
>
> Mrs. Madison was tall, large, and rather masculine in personal dimensions; her complexion was so fair and brilliant as to redeem this objection in its perfectly feminine beauty . . . [6]

The Madisons settled in the White House, and Dolley immediately set to redecorating. The White House was not quite ten years old, but Dolley favored bright colors to dull ones, and she got her way.

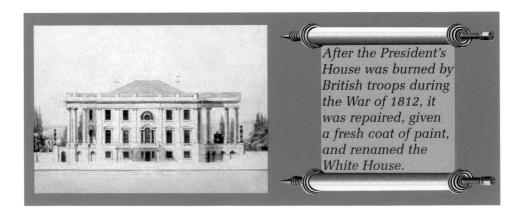

After the President's House was burned by British troops during the War of 1812, it was repaired, given a fresh coat of paint, and renamed the White House.

Once the redecorating was completed, Dolley hosted the first of her many social occasions. The men wore formal dress; the ladies appeared in elegant gowns. Social life in the White House ran smoothly; federal politics did not.

On the positive side, the government annexed West Florida after a rebellion by American settlers. Although the annexation took place in 1810, occupation of the land was not complete until 1813.

In Congress, Speaker of the House Nathaniel Macon proposed a series of laws dealing with trading with Great Britain. Strangely, one bill ceased trading with Britain and the other called to start up British trade again. The second measure allowed Britain free access to trading with American merchants. Considering the problems with British seizure of American ships, the bills left both Congress and the American people confused.

Congress created further problems for Madison. The renewal of the national bank charter was rejected. Requests for more money for the army were approved, but money for the navy was refused. Madison tried to gear up for war with Great Britain, which he felt was inevitable. Congress fought him all the way, yet changed positions when ship seizures, cargo losses, and human costs became too great to ignore.

In June 1812, Madison asked for and got a declaration of war against Great Britain. Among his reasons for going to war was that "British cruisers have been in the practice also of violating the rights and the peace of our coasts. They hover over and harass our entering and departing commerce . . . and have wantonly spilt American blood."[7] Although his health was poor, Madison played an active role in all aspects of the war effort. He ran for a second term as president and again defeated DeWitt Clinton.

The American navy, inexperienced and badly supplied, provided rare highlights in the early part of the war. Victories on Lake Erie forced the British to withdraw from Detroit. Another victory at the battle of the Thames resulted in the death of a Shawnee chief, Tecumseh, who was head of the Indian confederation of the northwest (Ohio, Michigan, Illinois, and Indiana). At the same time, the British navy extended its blockade of the East Coast from the Chesapeake up to New York.

An 1873 painting by William Henry Powell of the battle of Lake Erie depicts the U.S. victory on September 10, 1813, that forced Britain to pull its troops out of Detroit and withdraw to Canada.

Madison knew that war was never a permanent solution. In 1814, he appointed John Quincy Adams, James Bayard, Henry Clay, Jonathan Russell, and Albert Gallatin to negotiate peace with Great Britain. While they negotiated, the British invaded and burned key buildings in Washington, D.C. The Americans, in turn, saw victories at Lake Champlain and Baltimore. Finally the negotiators reached an agreement and signed a peace treaty at Ghent on December 24, 1814. The treaty restored captured lands to their original owners. Early in 1815, before news of the treaty reached the troops, the Americans defeated the British at the battle of New Orleans. Two weeks later, the Senate voted to approve the treaty. The war was officially over.

Before the end of his term, Madison changed his former stance and promoted the idea of a national bank. Congress initiated tariffs to protect American businesses. Indiana became a state. Two years later, James Monroe was elected president, and Madison left office. It was 1817, and Madison had turned sixty-six years old; it was time to retire.

First Lady Dolley Madison

Dolley Payne was born in 1768 to John and Mary Payne. Her parents were members of the Society of Friends, often referred to as Quakers. Dolley was born in North Carolina, but moved to Philadelphia when she was about five.

Dolley was raised following the strict rules of the Society's teachings. She was, nonetheless, lighthearted, happy, and outgoing. She had bright blue eyes, dark curly hair, and a fair complexion. By all accounts, she was considered very attractive.

When Dolley was about twenty-two years old, she married a young lawyer, John Todd Jr. Their marriage was brief; John died of yellow fever just three years later, and their three-month-old son William Isaac Todd died on the same day. At twenty-five, Dolley was a widow and a mother to William's older brother, Payne Todd.

As a young widow, Dolley Madison attracted the attention of many single men who came to Philadelphia. The city served as the United States capital and site of the United States Congress. Among the young men attracted to Dolley was James Madison, representative from Virginia.

The relationship seemed impossible. He was seventeen years older than she. He was serious and bookish, while she was fun-loving and engaging. He was Episcopalian, and she was Quaker. Despite these differences, the couple married in 1794.

Dolley quickly became the center of social occasions. She gave up the strict dress code of the Quakers and became an admired fashion plate. Margaret Bayard Smith, a follower of government social events, said of Dolley, "She looked a Queen. . . . It would be absolutely impossible for anyone to behave with more perfect propriety than she did."[8]

Once Madison retired from public office, he and Dolley returned to Montpelier, their Virginia home. Their financial situation was grim, and after Madison died in 1836, Dolley had to sell the family home to survive. Dolley Madison died in 1849 in Washington, D.C.

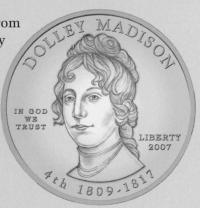

For Your Information

Shown around six years before his death, Madison was still active in politics, but pain in his joints had slowed him down significantly. Madison spent decades in tireless service to his country. His political vision carved out a strong and free United States.

CHAPTER
5

A Lasting Legacy

It was surprising how popular James Madison was when he left office. Critics complained that he had led the United States into a war for which it was not prepared. The military had been weak, generals were incompetent, and the navy remained poorly supplied. The British were still in Canada; foreign trade was still struggling. Yet Madison could not have been more popular.

Former President John Adams offered his opinion of why Madison's administration had been a success despite waging another expensive war:

Mr. Madison's administration has proved great points, long disputed in Europe and America:
1. He has proved that an administration, under our present Constitution, can declare war.
2. That it can make peace.
3. That, money or no money, government or no government, Great Britain can never conquer this country or any considerable part of it.
4. That our officers and men by land are equal to any [British forces] . . .
5. That our navy is equal . . . to any that ever floated on the ocean.[1]

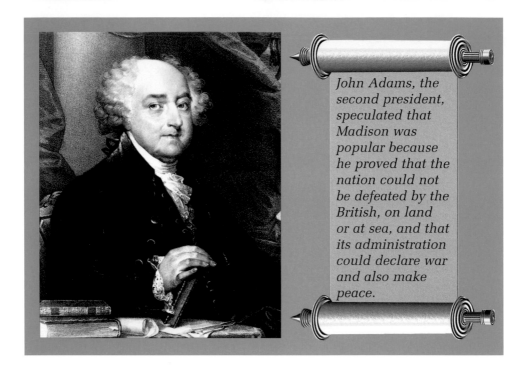

John Adams, the second president, speculated that Madison was popular because he proved that the nation could not be defeated by the British, on land or at sea, and that its administration could declare war and also make peace.

Madison was sixty-six years old when Monroe took over the presidency. His wife Dolley was only forty-nine. The pair retired to Montpelier, much against Dolley's wishes. After eight years in Washington serving the nation, she wanted a European vacation. Paris, in particular, had great appeal. James was more practical. Money was tight; he did not intend to waste any on frivolous vacations.

Madison intended to take up his former life as a gentleman farmer. His old friend Thomas Jefferson had a different idea. It had long been Jefferson's dream to found a university. He asked Madison to hold a seat on the first Board of Visitors at Jefferson's University of Virginia in Charlottesville. Madison helped Jefferson set up the school's curriculum and hire the faculty. Classes began in 1825, a year before Jefferson died on July 4, 1826.

As part of Jefferson's will, Madison inherited Jefferson's favorite gold-decorated walking stick. Madison was touched by this gift from his longtime friend. The walking stick was, he said, "a token of the place I held in the friendship of one whom I so much revered and

Madison's beloved Montpelier, shown here under major reconstruction, covers 2,650 acres in Virginia. Today archaeological digs are offering insight into the lives of the Madison family and the enslaved African Americans who worked on the estate. Montpelier is open to paying visitors.

loved when living, and whose memory can never cease to be dear to me."[2]

Madison followed Jefferson as rector of the university. Whenever Madison and his wife visited the university, they walked together on the grounds. Dolley was still young and in good health. Madison, shorter and thinner, was slower in pace but still alert and capable. He did his best for the university, while at Montpelier drought and low crop prices ate away at his finances.

In 1829 Madison was elected to the Virginia convention for revising the state constitution. Madison was the only one who had

attended the original state and federal constitutional conventions. The Virginia delegates fought over voting district boundaries. Tidewater districts wanted to count slaves when determining the population in each district. The Piedmont districts to the west felt they had less representation because they had fewer slaves. Madison tried to negotiate a compromise that would have all districts represented fairly, but no one listened.

Age caught up with Madison. His joints ached from rheumatism, and he had to stop writing and walking. By 1834, he had to give up being rector of the university. On June 28, 1836, Madison died at Montpelier. Just before his death, he dictated his final message to the nation:

> As this advice, if it, ever see the light, will not do so till I am no more, it may be considered as issuing from the tomb, where truth alone can be respected, and the happiness of man alone consulted. It will be entitled, therefore, to whatever weight can be derived from good intentions, and from the experience of one who has served his country in various stations through a period of forty years; who espoused in his youth, and adhered through his life, to the cause of its liberty. . . .[3]

Madison was the last of the Founding Fathers to pass away. His legacy was a democratic government set up in the Constitution. He ensured the freedoms of individual citizens written in the Bill of Rights. Once freedom from Great Britain had been achieved, James Madison's governmental vision carved out a strong United States of America.

Thomas Jefferson

Thomas Jefferson was one of James Madison's closest friends throughout his adult life. Both men came from the Piedmont region of Virginia, and enjoyed a warm, close friendship, in and out of politics.

Jefferson was born in 1743 in Albemarle County, Virginia. His family was wealthy and among the social elite of colonial Virginia. When his father died, Jefferson inherited 5,000 acres of land. A gifted architect and writer, he decided to design and build his own home—Monticello—which he began when he was only twenty-six. Three years later, he married Martha Wayles Skelton, a widow. The couple had six children, but four of them died young. Jefferson owned not only the partially built Monticello, but also other plantations in Albemarle and Bedford counties. Monticello was a typical plantation-style estate.

Jefferson was a respected lawyer, local magistrate (judge), a member of the Virginia House of Burgesses, and state governor. He represented Virginia at the Continental Congress and wrote the draft of the Declaration of Independence. In 1785, he became the United States ambassador to France. Within a few years, he became the vice-president of the United States, and then the president. During his presidency, Jefferson bought a block of land from France—the Louisiana Purchase—that doubled the size of the young United States.

After leaving office, Jefferson founded the University of Virginia, designing several of its buildings. He faced financial ruin and ended up having to sell his extensive library to the government for the Library of Congress. It was Jefferson's personal library that replaced the books burned by the British in the War of 1812.

Jefferson and John Adams died on the same day. Symbolically, the two great Founding Fathers both died on July 4, 1826, the fiftieth anniversary of the nation's first Independence Day.

Chronology

1751 James Madison Jr. is born on March 16 at Montpelier, Virginia.

1762 Madison begins attending boarding school.

1769 Madison enters the College of New Jersey at Princeton.

1775 Orange County, Virginia, militia is raised and drilled by Madison.

1776 Madison becomes a delegate to the Virginia convention.

1779 Madison becomes a delegate to the Continental Congress.

1782 Virginia elects Madison to Congress.

1789 Madison suggests the United States adopt a Bill of Rights.

1790 Madison attends the second session of the First Federal Congress.

1794 Dolley Payne Todd and James Madison marry on September 15.

1804 Madison protests the British practice of impressment.

1809 Madison takes the oath of office as president on March 4.

1810 A proclamation issued by Madison annexes the territory of West Florida.

1812 The United States declares war against Great Britain.

1814 British attack Washington, D.C., and burn the White House. War ends with the signing of the Treaty of Ghent.

1816 Madison signs a bill establishing a national bank.

1817 Dolley and James Madison retire to Montpelier.

1819 Madison attends the first meeting of the Board of Visitors of the University of Virginia.

1825 Crop failures, bad weather, and falling prices cause Madison financial trouble.

1826 Madison becomes rector of the University of Virginia.

1829 Madison attends the Virginia state constitutional convention.

1831 Trouble with rheumatism prevents Madison from writing or walking.

1833 Madison becomes the honorary president of the American Colonization Society.

1834 Madison retires as rector of the University of Virginia.

1836 James Madison dies at Montpelier on June 28. He is buried on the property.

Timeline in History

1715   Tea is introduced to the colonies.

1719   Daniel Defoe publishes the book *Robinson Crusoe.*

1725   Catherine becomes empress of Russia.

1750   The waltz becomes a popular dance in Europe.

1754   The French and Indian War begins in North America.

1770   Thomas Gainsborough paints the picture *Blue Boy.*

1773   Captain Cook becomes the first person to sail across the Antarctic Circle.

1775   Daniel Boone blazes the Wilderness Road through the Allegheny Mountains.

1781   William Herschel discovers the planet Uranus.

1783   Mongolfier brothers make the first manned flight in a hot air balloon.

1787   Wolfgang Amadeus Mozart writes the opera *Don Giovanni.*

1793   Eli Whitney invents the cotton gin.

1796   Doctor Edward Jenner develops a vaccine against smallpox.

1803   The Napoleonic War begins between Great Britain and France.

1804   The Lewis and Clark Expedition explore the newly purchased Louisiana Territory.

1807   Beethoven completes his Fifth Symphony.

1812   Napoleon invades Russia.

1813   Uncle Sam becomes the symbol of the United States.

1818   Mary Wollstonecroft Shelley writes the novel *Frankenstein.*

1821   Cherokee leader Sequoyah develops a written language for his people.

1829   Louis Braille develops a system of writing for the blind.

1831   Cyrus McCormick invents a mechanical reaper.

1833   General Santa Anna becomes president of Mexico.

1838   Samuel Morse develops the Morse code for telegraphy.

1844   French author Alexandre Dumas publishes *The Three Musketeers.*

Chapter Notes

Chapter 1. A Wartime President

1. James Morton Smith, ed., *The Republic of Letters: The Correspondence Between Thomas Jefferson and James Madison 1776–1826, Vol. III* (New York: W. W. Norton & Company, 1995), p. 1687.

2. James D. Richardson, ed., *James Madison: A Compilation of the Messages and Papers of the Presidents* (Whitefish, Mont.: Kessinger Publishing), 2004, p. 47.

Chapter 2. A Childhood of Privilege

1. Ralph Ketcham, *James Madison: A Biography* (Charlottesville, Va.: University Press of Virginia, 1990), p. 28.

Chapter 3. From Revolution to the Bill of Rights

1. James Morton Smith, ed., *The Republic of Letters: The Correspondence Between Thomas Jefferson and James Madison 1776–1826, Vol. I* (New York: W. W. Norton & Company, 1995), p. 38.

2. James Madison, and Adrienne Koch, ed., *Notes of Debates in the Federal Convention of 1787* (New York: W. W. Norton & Company, 1966), pp. xi–xii.

3. William Lee Miller, *The Business of May Next: James Madison and the Founding* (Charlottesville, Va.: University Press of Virginia, 1992), p. 235.

4. Ibid., p. 237.

5. Smith, p. 592.

6. Thomas Head, ed., *The Bill of Rights* (Farmington Hills, Mich.: Greenhaven Press, 2004), p. 58.

7. "A History of the Bill of Rights," www.aclu.org/printer/printer.php

Chapter 4. The Nation's Fourth President

1. James Morton Smith, ed., *The Republic of Letters: The Correspondence Between Thomas Jefferson and James Madison 1776–1826, Vol. II* (New York: W. W. Norton & Company, 1995), p. 847.

2. Ibid., p. 1258.

3. James D. Richardson, ed., *James Madison: A Compilation of the Messages and Papers of the Presidents* (Whitefish, Mont.: Kessinger Publishing), 2004, p. 4.

4. Ibid., p. 5.

5. Smith, *Letters, Vol. III,* p. 1562.

6. Ibid., p. 1563.

7. Richardson, p. 48.

8. "Dolley Payne Todd Madison," www.whitehouse.gov/history/firstladies/dm4.html

Chapter 5. A Lasting Legacy

1. Garry Wills, *James Madison* (New York: Henry Holt and Company, 2002), p. 157.

2. James Morton Smith, ed., *The Republic of Letters: The Correspondence Between Thomas Jefferson and James Madison 1776–1826, Vol. III* (New York: W. W. Norton & Company, 1995), p. 1974.

3. Ibid., p. 2002.

Further Reading

For Young Adults

Cunningham, Alvin Robert. *Washington Is Burning! The War of 1812.* Logan, Iowa: Perfection Learning, 2003.

Freedman, Russell. *In Defense of Liberty: The Story of America's Bill of Rights.* New York: Holiday House, 2003.

Kozleski, Lisa. *James Madison (Childhoods of the Presidents).* Broomall, Pennsylvania: Mason Crest Publishing, 2002.

Mitchell, Barbara. *Father of the Constitution: A Story About James Madison.* Minneapolis: Carolrhoda, 2004.

Santella, Andrew. *James Madison (Profiles of the Presidents).* Mankato, Minnesota: Compass Point Press, 2002.

———. *The War of 1812.* Danbury, Connecticut: Children's Press, 2000.

Venezia, Mike. *James Madison: Fourth President, 1809–1817.* Danbury, Connecticut: Children's Press, 2004.

Weatherly, Myra. *Dolley Madison: America's First Lady.* Greensboro, North Carolina: Morgan Reynolds Publishing, 2003.

Works Consulted

Carey, Charles W., ed. *The American Revolution.* Farmington Hills, Michigan: Greenhaven Press, 2004.

Head, Tom, ed. *The Bill of Rights.* Farmington Hills, Michigan: Greenhaven Press, 2004.

Ketcham, Ralph. *James Madison.* Charlottesville: University Press of Virginia, 1990.

Madison, James. *The Constitutional Convention: A Narrative History from the Notes of James Madison.* New York: Modern Library, 2005.

———. *United States Constitutional Convention* (1787). New York: W. W. Norton & Company, 1966.

Miller, William Lee. *The Business of May Next: James Madison and the Founding.* Charlottesville: University Press of Virginia, 1992.

Rakove, Jack N. *James Madison: Writings.* New York: The Library of America, 1999.

Further Reading

Smith, James Morton, ed. *The Republic of Letters: The Correspondence Between Thomas Jefferson and James Madison 1776–1826, vols. 1–3.* New York: W. W. Norton & Company, 1995.

Wills, Garry. *James Madison.* New York: Henry Holt and Company, 2002.

On the Internet

American President: James Madison, Miller Center of Public Affairs
http://www.millercenter.virginia.edu/academic/americanpresident/madison

James Madison, The White House
www.whitehouse.gov/history/presidents/jm4.html

The Bill of Rights, Archiving Early America
http://www.earlyamerica.com/earlyamerica/freedom/bill/

James Madison's Montpelier
www.montpelier.org/

James Madison Museum
www.jamesmadisonmus.org/

The James Madison Papers, The Library of Congress
http://memory.loc.gov/ammem/collections/madison_papers/

James Madison, The Internet Public Library
www.ipl.org/div/potus/jmadison.html

Glossary

activist (AK-tih-vist)
A person who actively supports one side or another of a controversial issue.

adherence (ad-HEER-ents)
Loyalty to a religion, cause, or political party.

amendment (uh-MEND-ment)
An addition or change to an official document.

annexation (aa-nek-SAY-shun)
The addition of a parcel of land.

battery (BAAT-teh-ree)
A fortress or group of cannons.

bondage (BON-dij)
Slavery.

confederation (kon-feh-deh-RAY-shun)
A league or group with similar interests.

constitution (kon-stih-TOO-shun)
A document that sets out the formation of a government.

currency (KER-en-see)
The money used by a nation.

fallow (FAA-loh)
Left unplanted.

hypochondriac (hy-poh-KON-dree-ak)
Someone who complains of being ill when they are not.

impressment (im-PRESS-ment)
The act of seizing men and forcing them to work on a ship against their will.

piedmont (PEED-mont)
The foothills of a mountain range.

plantation (plan-TAY-shun)
A type of farm on which one major crop is grown, such as cotton or tobacco.

rector (REK-tur)
The head of a university or school.

republic (ree-PUB-lik)
A government with a chief of state that is usually a president, but never a monarch.

revolution (reh-vuh-LOO-shun)
A formal act of rebelling against a current government.

rheumatism (ROO-muh-tih-zem)
A painful condition that affects muscles and joints.

tidewater (TYD-wah-tur)
A lowland coastal region, often featuring marsh or swamps.

Index